THOROUGHBREDS

BY
DOROTHY M. CALLAHAN

EDITED BY
DR. HOWARD SCHROEDER
Professor In Reading and Language Arts
Dept. of Elementary Education
Mankato State University

DESIGNED & PRODUCED BY
BAKER STREET PRODUCTIONS
MANKATO, MINNESOTA

COVER GRAPHICS BY
BOB WILLIAMS

CRESTWOOD HOUSE
Mankato, Minnesota

LIBRARY OF CONGRESS CATALOGING IN PUBLICATION DATA
Callahan, Dorothy M.
  Thoroughbreds.

  (Horses, pasture to paddock)
  SUMMARY: Discusses the breed of horses known as thoroughbred and follows a
new colt from birth to the day of its maiden race.
  1. Thoroughbred horse--Juvenile literature. 2. Horse-racing--Juvenile literature.
(1. Thoroughbred horse. 2. Race horses. 3. Horse racing) I. Schroeder, Howard. II.
Title. III. Series.
SF293.T5C33   1983   636.1'32   83-7731
ISBN 0-89686-232-1

International Standard Book Numbers:	**Library of Congress Catalog Card Number:**
Library Binding 0-89686-232-1	83-7731

PHOTOGRAPH CREDITS

Cappy Jackson: Cover
Alix Coleman: 5, 12, 17, 21, 25, 26, 28, 29, 31, 32, 35, 37, 38, 42
Wide World: 7
Keeneland Library: 8, 11
Bob Williams: 14
Joe Berke: 18
New York Racing Association: 22, 39, 41, 44

CRESTWOOD HOUSE

Hwy. 66 South, Box 3427
Mankato, MN 56002-3427

TABLE
OF
CONTENTS

Dedicated to Kathy, for her inspiration; to Frank, for his information; to Charlsie, for her verification.

①
A THOROUGHBRED
IS BORN

It is March, a time of new beginnings on the breeding farm. A dark brown mare lies on her side in the fresh straw of the foaling barn. A man stands just outside the stall, quietly watching. The foaling man will help Chocolate bring her baby into the world. But he will help only if he is needed.

This is Chocolate's fifth foal, or baby. Her three colts, or male horses, have been winners at the race track. Her only filly, or female horse, is just starting its training. Mother horses, or broodmares, have a foal nearly every year. They carry them inside their bodies for eleven months.

Chocolate gives a great sigh as the foal's head begins to appear. The head is tucked between its forelegs as it should be. Now the rest of the foal emerges and the foaling man sees that the baby is a colt or male baby. The foal kicks at pieces of the filmy sac still around him. It was a protective cover inside his mother and now he wants it off.

Like all horses before him, he feels nature's call to get to his feet. If he had been born in the wilderness, an enemy may have struck at any time. Within hours of his birth, he would have had to run with the herd.

There is fossil evidence that an early horse called

Eohippus lived in North America thousands of years ago. It was only ten inches tall and ran on three toes. Our present day *Equus* has become a much larger animal with great speed. It has one toe, called a hoof.

Chocolate's new colt will probably grow to the size of his father, Malta. Horse size is measured in the width of hands from the ground to the withers. (An area above the shoulders). Each hand equals four inches. Malta stands sixty-four inches (1.6 meters) tall, or sixteen hands.

Chocolate begins to get up in her stall. She nudges her little one and her rough, dry tongue licks his small nose. The nose must be cleared so that he can

The day's activities begin early at a breeding farm.

breathe properly. A horse cannot fill its lungs through its mouth.

Now the foaling man comes near. With soothing words, he talks to Chocolate as he gently dries off her baby. Then he waits for the foal to stand. The man is patient and lets nature do its job.

Three times the little colt tries to stand but topples back. On the fourth attempt, he gets to his feet. He wants breakfast and nature has told him where to go. Chocolate stands quietly as her new foal nurses.

Seeing that all is well, the foaling man leaves to get some nourishing grain for Chocolate. But first he stops at the office to make a record of the foal's birth. The record must list the colt's name, his father, his mother and his mother's father. A thorough-bred's family tree is traced down the mother's side.

The foaling man writes: "a bay colt by Malta out of Chocolate by Cocoa Bean." Soon the foal's owner will apply for his registration with the Jockey Club, which keeps all birth records. If accepted, his name will be official — Chocolate Malt.

② A NEW BREED

Chocolate Malt is a thoroughbred which is a breed of horse that dates back three hundred years. At that time, English horses were bred with horses from the eastern Mediterranean area.

Nashua's son — This colt is the first offspring sired by Nashua, the world-leading, money-winning thoroughbred in 1958.

English horses, and those of all Northern Europe, were called cold-blooded. Many were descended from animals that carried knights in armor into battle. They were strong and could survive cold winters.

In the Asian and North African lands that border the eastern Mediterranean Sea, the horses were called warm-blooded. These horses, known as Arabians, could withstand the dry heat of the desert areas.

Since 2000 B.C., the desert people had tamed and bred their Arabian horses to be fast, hardy and

(Top) Byerly Turk, (center) Darley Arabian, and (bottom) Godolphin Arabian.

beautiful. Many tribes had won battles riding into enemy camps on their four-legged "secret weapons."

British horse owners wanted to improve the speed of their northern horses through breeding, or mating, them with Arabians. But the Middle Eastern people did not want to part with their horses. In some countries, it was a crime to sell an Arabian mare to a foreigner. Stallions, or male horses, were easier to obtain, but they were very expensive.

Three of these horses, the Byerly Turk, the Darley Arabian, and the Godolphin Arabian were brought to England and bred to English horses.

Captain Byerly, a British Army officer captured a sleek, dark colt while fighting in Turkey in 1688. He used him as a war horse, then retired him to England. There, this horse became known as the Byerly Turk.

In 1704, Thomas Darley was doing business for Queen Anne in Syria. He secretly bought a pure Arabian colt and slipped him out of the country. This colt became known as the Darley Arabian.

Mystery surrounds the early life of the Godolphin Arabian. It was sent as a gift to King Louis of France from the Sultan of Morocco. Somehow the horse ended up on a Paris street being used as a cart horse. It was rescued by a Quaker gentlemen, Jethro Coke. In 1724, the horse arrived at the stables of the Earl of Godolphin.

The offspring of these three stallions were faster and stronger than the native English horses.

Through the eighteenth century, this breed, now called the thoroughbred, began to develop. It was the offspring of these three imported Arabians who became the founding fathers of the thoroughbred breed. Three of these offspring — Matchem, Herod, and Eclipse — became important race horses.

Matchem, grandson of the Godolphin Arabian, raced successfully for ten years. He began his career at the age of five, as many horses did in those days. Since races were run in parts called heats, each four miles long, a horse needed to be fully grown to compete. Often only two horses raced at once. The winner had to win two out of three heats. If the heat ended in a tie, called a "dead heat," it had to be run again. Sometimes the horses had to run sixteen or twenty miles before the match was over.

In 1758, Herod, a grandson of the Byerly Turk was born. A large brown horse, he had a long, arched neck and powerful shoulders. His strong rump muscles made him a faster runner than his grandfather.

Herod raced only five times and won three. His greatness was in his offspring. He sired, or was the father of, 497 winning horses. It is said that between 1775 and 1800, his offspring won half of all races they ran.

Eclipse was born on April 1, 1764, under the bad

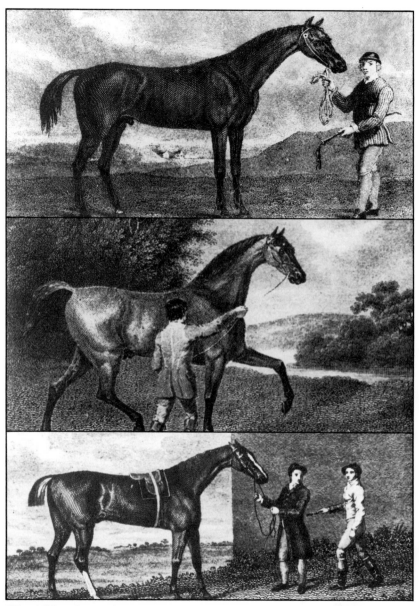

(Top) Matchem, (center) King Herod, and (bottom) Eclipse.

"Cooling out" — A horse has to be cooled down after running.

omen of a total eclipse. The foal seemed an April Fool's joke. He was an ugly, too-tall chestnut, or reddish-colored horse. He had a high white stocking on one leg and a wide white strip, or blaze, on his nose.

Eclipse grew up seeming to hate all other creatures. He nipped at horses and tossed men who tried to ride him. But when he finally came to the track, no horse ever passed him.

Eclipse raced for only eighteen months but came in first all twenty-six times at the track. Eight of those victories were called "walkovers." In these races the opponent never showed up, and Eclipse just had to walk over the course to win. There was a saying, "Eclipse first, the rest nowhere" to describe how he ran. But it fit his ability as a sire even better.

Eclipse retired to a farm after his racing career. The four hundred foals he sired won 344 races.

By the early nineteenth century, the offspring of Matchem, Herod and Eclipse were the greatest horses in England. All owners wanted foals with their bloodlines.

So the English wrote a book called the **General Stud Book.** It includes only horses which could trace their history back to these three. So Matchem, Herod and Eclipse became known as the foundation sires, or fathers, of the thoroughbred breed.

The **American Stud Book** has the same requirement. Ninety-eight percent of all horses racing in the United States today trace their bloodlines back to Eclipse.

BREEDING

Forty thousand thoroughbreds are born each year. Only one can be the Eclipse Award, or best, Horse of the Year. But on this day of Chocolate Malt's birth, his owner and breeder think he could get the award someday. In bringing Chocolate Malt's parents together, they followed an old horse breeder's saying: "Breed the best to the best and hope for the best."

The colt's father, Malta, was known as a stayer, or a winner of long distance races. But he was nervous and hard to train.

When she raced, Chocolate Malt's mother was a sprinter. Her wide chest and heavily-muscled rump made her a winner at short distances. She also had a very gentle nature.

In the mating of Malta and Chocolate, the breeders hoped to get the best qualities of each in their foal.

YEARLING SALES

Chocolate Malt is a fit young colt. He is called a homebred. His owner bred the colt to race for his own stable of horses. Not all owners breed horses to keep. They often sell the one-year-old offspring of their mares at yearling sales.

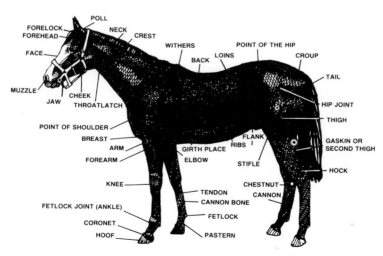

Before the bidding begins, stable owners and their trainers look at each young horse carefully. They check a booklet which lists the family history going back many generations. The bidding often goes over $100,000. Some colts may even sell for several million dollars. When buyers risk this much money in an untrained animal, they have to know a great deal about what makes a good racehorse.

③
THE THOROUGHBRED'S BODY

The color of a horse is decided by checking the hairs of its coat. Most thoroughbreds are called bays, a yellowish tan to dark auburn shade. Their mane, tail and lower legs are black. Other thoroughbreds are chestnuts, browns, grays, or roans. A chestnut is golden yellow to deep liver, with similar colored mane and tail. A dark brown horse can almost look black. A gray horse has a mixture of black and white hairs. A roan is red and white.

SIZE AND SPEED

A racehorse can weigh anywhere from 900 to 1200 pounds (408-544 kg) and stand about sixteen hands tall. Trainers have a saying: "A horse is too large or too small only if it can't run fast enough or far enough.

Through thousands of years of development, a horse's body has been fashioned for flight. The cheetah has a faster burst of speed. But the horse is the fastest animal in the world at a distance of a mile. It can run thirty-five to forty miles an hour.

CONFORMATION

A horse's body balance and general good looks are called its conformation. The animal should stand squarely on all four straight legs. Its head should be set on a long, slender neck. The horse should have a full chest that has space for a large heart and lungs — both are necessary when the horse is in full flight.

SENSORY ORGANS

Wide nostrils are important since a horse cannot breathe through it's mouth. Some horses break blood vessels in their nose when they run hard. The blood might be inhaled into their lungs, choking them and slowing them down. In certain states medicine can be given to stop this condition. But in others like New York, a "bleeder" may not race until the track veterinarian sees that its nose has healed naturally.

Everyone wants a horse with a "good eye." This

To keep a horse from jumping shadows, a shadow roll is put across the horse's nose. This horse is also wearing blinders.

means one which is alert and curious. A fiery eye can be a sign of a bad temper.

A horse's eyes are a bluish-brown color. They stick out from its head. This is so a horse can see all around its body without moving. But each eye sees a different view. The horse's brain does not blend these two views into one picture as a human brain would. Only special training teaches a horse to focus ahead on the track. If side vision still distracts the horse, a trainer may use blinders. These are leather cups placed next to the eyes so the animal can only see straight ahead.

A horse cannot focus on things closer than four feet (1.2 m). Objects which suddenly come into view may scare the horse. A trainer may put a shadow roll, or fur band, across the horse's nose, to keep it from jumping over shadows.

A horse can rotate its ears in half circles to pick up sounds. Because a horse's hearing is so good, sudden noises can cause alarm.

FEET

The foot is an enlarged, single toe. It is covered with a hoof, or hard surface, that has no feeling and grows like a human fingernail. The hoof absorbs the

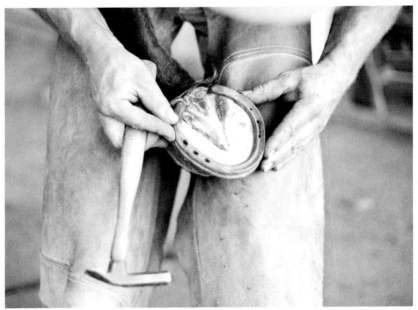

A farrier puts on new horseshoes.

half-ton weight of a horse by expanding when it touches the ground. When picked up, the hoof returns to its original shape.

A farrier, or blacksmith, trims the horse's hooves, and puts "shoes" on them. Aluminum horse shoes are factory-made in all sizes. But if a horse has an unusual hoof, it must have a special shoe. These shoes are made in an open fire, as they have been for centuries. The fire softens the horseshoe so it can be bent to fit the horse's hoof.

STOMACH

A racehorse lives a controlled life. Its food is served three times a day with the big meal in the afternoon. It has a balance of oats, bran, corn, carrots, molasses and vitamin pellets.

The horse has sharp front teeth for biting and grazing. Powerful jaws and back molars grind its food.

The horse's digestive system is very delicate. A horse's stomach is like a human's with one big difference. A horse cannot burp or vomit. So gases, poisons, or too much food and water can be trapped inside. This causes colic which is a severe stomach-ache from which a horse can die. Often, only an operation can save its life.

TEMPERAMENT

Because thoroughbreds are bred for speed and power, they are often nervous and high-strung. Trainers must be patient and kind. The quicker a trainer can learn his horse's personality, the happier both will be.

④
GETTING READY TO RACE

By September, Chocolate Malt is six months old. The stable workers now call him Malty. He is growing big on grain and pasture grass. It is time to take him from Chocolate and her milk. He must become a weanling.

In the past, all foals on a farm used to be separated from their mothers on "weaning day." This led to much crying and crashing about as mare and foal looked for each other.

Now there is a new method. Only two or three mares and foals are separated each day. They are taken to fields at opposite ends of the farm where other foals and mares are still together. This family setting seems to calm the horses quicker.

So on a late summer morning, Malty sees Chocolate for the last time. Malty is led by himself to their usual pasture. For a while he runs wildly, looking for his mother. Then he finds a few weanlings who want to play and the games take his mind off his mother.

But when he gets hungry, he begins to whinny for Chocolate. When she doesn't come, he looks around. Soon he spies the foal creep. The creep is a feeding stall, built so low that only foals can fit in to nibble grain. Malty fills his stomach then races off to look for another playmate. His weaning is going well.

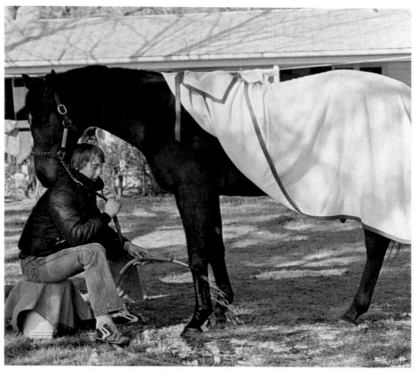

A horse's leg being hosed down after a workout.

AN OFFICIAL THOROUGHBRED

Chocolate Malt becomes a yearling on January 1, even though he has been alive for only nine months. All thoroughbreds change age on that day. This keeps them in groups that will race against each other.

Chocolate Malt's name is now official. It was accepted by the Jockey Club in August. It met their rules for registration. Chocolate Malt was not the name of a famous racehorse, or a horse that was still racing. The name was also not more than the legal eighteen spaces long. Now Malty's name as well as all his markings, are listed in the **American Stud Book.** Before Malty races, a registration number will

This young filly has gotten used to wearing a halter.

be tatooed inside his upper lip. This will keep another horse from ever running in his place.

EARLY TRAINING

Malty spends the spring and summer running free with other colts his age. It seems like fun to him but it is really his first training. The quick turning motions and bursts of speed all help to build strong muscles and alertness.

Malty has worn a halter since he was two weeks old. He has been led, brushed and groomed by people. He has learned to trust them. Now his trust will be tested.

In October, two men come into his stall. One holds a soft blanket to Malty's nose. He smells it. Then it is laid across Malty's back and he is walked.

Day by day more equipment is added. The trainers must be very patient. Finally Malty accepts a saddle. Next, a young man lays across the saddle. Malty can see his head out of one eye, his feet out of the other. Another man holding the reins watches for any sign of trouble. Malty is a good learner. Soon the young man is sitting in the saddle. Before long they go out on the soft dirt of the training track.

It will be a while before Malty is allowed to run fast. His young bones are still not fully-grown and strong.

HIS TRAINER

In January Malty is two years old. He meets Don, the trainer who has come to Kentucky from New York to make a racehorse out of him.

Malty's trainer has a plan. "We'll let him work down here for the winter," he tells the farm manager. "Then we'll take him to Belmont Park in New York. If he learns to run well, he can get in a few summer races there. Then we'll go upstate to Saratoga. That's where we'll see if he's good enough to 'run for the roses' in next year's Derby."

Every trainer and owner wants a horse good enough to run in the Kentucky Derby. It is the country's biggest race for three-year-olds.

LIFE ON THE BACKSTRETCH

When the first blades of grass begin to peek through the ground, a van backs up to Malty's barn to take him to Belmont Park. Malty will not be back to the farm until his racing career is over.

The colt quickly adjusts to life on the Belmont Park backstretch — the stable area on the far side of the track.

Each morning Malty's exercise rider, Joanne, takes him onto the track. He has begun a "legging-up" program. This is an eight-week series of slow

An exercise girl is getting a "leg up."

gallops and walks that end in a two-mile run.

Next the speed training begins. Malty is allowed to breeze, or run fast, under his rider's tight control.

After a workout, Malty is unsaddled, hosed down with water and turned over to a "hot walker." This person walks him until he is cooled down. This is a very important part of the running process. A horse's heartrate and breathing must be slowly returned to normal.

As Malty returns to the barn area, Don watches him carefully. He looks at the horses legs to see if there is any swelling.

MALTY'S GROOM

While he has been out on the track, Malty's closest companion, Karen, has been changing his bedding of straw. Karen has been cleaning stalls since she got her first pony. Now she does it for pay.

Karen has been Malty's groom since the day he came to Belmont. Don relies on Karen to teach the horse manners. She helps Malty's training by reporting things about his personality and learning style.

When Malty is finished walking, Karen sponges him with soap and water. Then she uses a hoof pick to clean his feet. She rubs his legs with ointment and puts on stall bandages. These wrappings keep the

Leg bandages are laundered and hung up to dry.

horse from bumping its legs in the twelve foot square stall.

Feeling clean and relaxed, Malty lies down in his stall and rolls back and forth in the new straw bedding. But this is no time for a nap. Though only 10:30 a.m., it is time for lunch. Breakfast was six long hours ago.

Malty gets to his feet and whinnies at Karen. He rattles his feed bucket with his nose.

Don feels Malty is a special horse. By trusting Karen to care for him, it shows that she is special, too. It is well-known around the track, that "the best grooms rub the best horses."

Before 1960, Karen could not have had this job. Women were not allowed to work on the backstretch. Now there are female grooms, hot walkers, exercise riders, jockeys and trainers.

Malty's exercise rider, Joanne, rode jumping horses in shows before coming to the track. When she gets a little more experience, she will apply for a jockey's license. Don has promised to let her ride for him.

SERIOUS TRAINING

Part of Malty's training takes place in the starting gate. An assistant starter begins the schooling by walking horses through the open doors of the gate. After they get used to the big gate, the front door is

An exercise girl is heading for a workout.

Starting gate doors are being opened and closed again and again.

closed, then the back one. The horses learn to rush off as soon as the front doors spring open.

Malty is beginning to train for a race. Don is happy with his size, power, and speed. He feels the horse will be able to run well in a six-furlong race.

A mile track is divided into eight-furlongs. Each furlong is an eighth of a mile. Red-and-white-striped poles with gold balls on top mark the furlongs. Black and white poles mark the half distances between. They are called the sixteenth poles.

Now that Malty is being prepared for a race, Don's regular jockey, Ted, rides him in the morning.

Today, Don wants to see how fast Malty can run three furlongs, or three-eighths of a mile. That is only half the distance of the race. But horses do not run at top speed for a whole race. Don just wants to check Malty's top speed.

TUNING UP
FOR THE RACE

It is 7:30 on a misty morning. Horses are warming up all over Belmont Park. Some are walking, others are jogging or breezing.

High above the finish line, in a glass booth, sit the clockers. They use special stopwatches to time horses in fifths of a second. Riders and horses wear no numbers or silks because this is not an official race. Clockers must know each horse's exercise rider or jockey.

The horse is a herd animal which means it feels safe in a pack. But winning racehorses must have the courage to run ahead of the pack. They must have the special quality that makes them want to lead.

Don feels Malty is a leader. He loves to run at full speed all the way to the finish line. Ted, Malty's jockey, has been trying to teach him to relax at the start and save his speed until he gets a signal.

On the far side of the track at the six-furlong pole, the starting gate is in place. Malty and Happiness Is, his stablemate since weanling days, are going to run together.

The doors spring open, and both are away with a quick burst of speed. The jockeys pull their reins tightly to slow the horses and teach them to save speed for later. The horses run side by side for the first two furlongs. Then, as planned, Happiness Is takes the lead. Ted holds Malty back by a length, the nose to rump measure of a horse.

As the two horses come out of the far turn, Ted feels Malty pulling to go faster. At the three-eighths pole, all the stopwatches click down. They begin timing Malty's top speed.

Ted eases his grip. Malty feels the signal and responds. He puts his head forward and digs his hoofs into the soft track. It takes only four strides for him to pass Happiness Is. The jockey crouches low

A trainer is clocking his horse.

Working out on the training track is necessary to condition the horse.

over Malty's withers as they leave the other horse far behind.

The clockers pop in their watch stems as Malty crosses the finish line. They smile and write the time on the morning's chart — thirty-five seconds.

Malty's time is very good. Out by the backstretch rail, Don's watch reads the same. He wants to smile, but he is afraid to do it yet. A trainer is a cautious person.

Don has seen many a "morning glory," or a horse that runs fast in a workout, but fades in an afternoon race. He has also seen many good horses break down, or seriously injure themselves.

Don will smile when Malty is the first to cross the finish line in a race.

THE RIGHT RACE

The Condition Book, which lists all the races for the next two weeks, has just been issued by the track Racing Secretary. Don opens it eagerly. He feels Malty is ready to run. Now he must find the right race for him.

It is the job of the Racing Secretary to design races for all the horses stabled at that track. It is like writing a play to suit the actors. The Racing Secretary wants every horse in every age and ability class to have a chance to come in first.

It is important for a trainer to know a horse's ability. A horse must not be raced against horses it has no chance to beat. Otherwise, it begins to think finishing with the pack is all right.

There are several kinds of races provided by the Racing Secretary. The Secretary sets the weight the horses must carry in order to give each one a chance to win. The weight consists of the jockey, saddle, and equipment. If more weight is needed, half-pound lead bars are added to a pad alongside the saddle.

An **allowance** race matches horses of similar age and ability at varying distances. A horse which has won fewer races is allowed to carry less weight.

In a **handicap** race, horses of greater ability must carry extra weight. These races are usually for three-year-old horses and older.

In a **weight-for-age** race, older horses must carry

more weight than younger ones, because they have more experience.

A **sweepstakes** (stakes) race is held for the best horses. It is the only kind of race in which an owner must pay a fee to have his horse compete. The winner gets a prize, or purse. This type of race dates back to the time when a horse would run to win a "purse". The purse was filled with the entrance fees paid by the horses' owners. Today, the track adds extra money too, and it is divided among the top runners in the race.

In a **claiming** race, the horses are actually for sale. An owner enters his horse in a race against other horses of equal value and ability. Any horse in the field may be bought for the price given that day by its owner. After the race, the owner may collect purse money, but another person can "claim," or buy, the horse.

Malty will run in a **maiden** race. It is a special contest for horses who have never won before. Usually run at short distances, it matches horses of the same sex and age and has them carrying the same weight.

⑤
RACE DAY

Malty paces back and forth in his stall. Every few minutes he whinnies.

Everything about today has broken his routine. After breakfast, he was walked instead of going to the track. Then the blacksmith came to give him new shoes. The hardest thing for Malty to understand was the tiny amount of oats in his lunch bucket. He rattled it until it went crashing to the ground.

It is Malty's first race day. If he stays on at the track, he will learn that shoes and a small amount of food mean a race.

The track veterinarian comes by to check Malty's health. He also draws out blood and takes a urine sample back to the laboratory to test. In New York State, a horse must be scratched, or taken out of the

Horses are groomed before a race at Saratoga.

race, if a drug of any kind is found in its system. In some states, drugs used for a medical reason are allowed.

Don arrives as Karen brings Malty out of the stall. The trainer bends down to check the horse's legs once more. "Well, this is it," he says to Karen. He points to number two in the program for the third race — Chocolate Malt. Karen smiles and begins brushing Malty's coat. She starts to feel nervous.

In a matter of minutes the backstretch microphone blares out. "Attention grooms. Please bring all horses for the third race to the paddock area."

Along the path, Karen and Malty pass two horses returning from the track. Their grooms do not look happy, as they talk softly to their sweating horses. Karen knows that the top finishers and any beaten favorites in each race must go to the laboratory shed to have another blood and urine test. These two horses have not gone to the shed.

JOCKEYS

While Karen and Malty are walking to the paddock, the jockeys are putting on their silks. These are shirts and caps in colors selected by the owner for his stable of horses. They are no longer made of silk, but man-made fibers that wash easily.

Some jockeys in the room today have ridden a thousand races. Others are still apprentices, or first-

Horses are going to the post before the start of the race.

These horses are going from the paddock to the track.

year riders. These new riders are called "bug boys," because they have an asterisk in the program next to their names that looks like a bug. Some of these "bug boys" are girls.

Pound for pound, jockeys are the strongest athletes in the world. They try to keep their weight down so they can at least "tack ten," or be 110 pounds while holding saddle and equipment. In that way they can ride the horses which are assigned low weights to carry. Jockeys who report to work overweight try to take pounds off in the sweatbox, or steam room.

Race riding is dangerous. A jockey runs the risk of

injury in every race. A horse can clip another's heels, break a bone or act wildly during a race. If a horse stumbles or falls, the jockey may be seriously hurt.

In a big stakes race, the jockey gets ten percent of the purse money. But in a small claiming or allowance race, a losing jockey may make as little as $30.00 for all the risk.

It is twenty minutes to the start of Malty's race. In the jockey's room, Ted slips on black and gold silks. His valet, or helper, has laid the silks out next to his pair of soft leather boots. The valet holds the tiny two-pound calfskin seat that is Ted's saddle. With it is a cloth with Malty's number, and the top girth that will go around both saddle and horse.

Holding his gear, Ted steps on the scale. "One-twelve," the Clerk of Scales says. That is the exact weight Malty and the other young horses in the

The buglar signals the horses to the post!

maiden race must carry. Because they have never won, the Racing Secretary makes their burden light.

Later in the day, Ted will ride an older horse who has won many races. Then he will have to add eighteen lead bars to a pocket alongside his saddle. That horse must carry one hundred thirty pounds. Other horses in the race with not as much experience carry six to twelve pounds less. This gives them a chance to beat the older horse, because its burden is heavier than theirs.

FINAL INSTRUCTIONS

"Come out, jocks." The riders walk to the paddock. Karen leads Malty into the saddling stall where Don is waiting. Don smooths out the cloth and lays the saddle on Malty. Karen pats his nose. Don puts his hand on Ted's shoulder. "Just ride him like the other morning. Keep him near the leader, then open up in the stretch."

"Put your riders up," says the Paddock Judge. Don cups his hands and reaches down to give Ted a leg-up. As they move off, Karen goes to the rail fence to watch the race with the rest of the grooms.

As the horses come onto the race track, the bugler comes out, too. In his traditional red and white hunt clothes, he faces the stands and plays "First Call." It is an old cavalry call to the parade grounds.

"The horses are on the track," the race announcer says.

The horses are out of the starting gate!

A car brings the Patrol Judges to their viewing points in towers around the track. Cameras will video tape the race to be sure no horse or jockey interferes with another.

When Malty comes out on the track, a lead pony walks with him. Tracks provide these companions for the horses to help keep them calm.

The announcer calls Malty's name and number as he passes the stands. Then Ted lets him jog off toward the starting gate which is set up just beyond the three-quarter pole. An assistant starter takes the reins of each horse, leading it into the gate. Malty's ears pick up the sounds as the other horses are loaded in with him. He seems to sense that this is not just practice. Ted grabs a handful of mane to keep from jerking backwards when Malty rushes from the starting gate.

Lead ponies are also used to calm the horses.

The Official Starter stands on a platform next to the gate. He has the gate release button in his hand. When he sees that all the horses are ready, he pushes it. The electric current that has held the doors closed is shut off. A loud bell rings and the doors spring open.

"And they're off," shouts the announcer.

The horses scramble for position. Jockeys try to follow their trainers' instructions. Ted tucks Malty into third place, holding him tightly.

Going into the far turn, the leaders begin to tire and fall back. Ted hears the jockey next to him start chirping to his horse. He lets that horse take the lead while he settles into second place.

At the final turn, called the stretch, the jockeys can hear the people in the grandstand screaming for their favorite horse. With a quarter-mile to go, it is time for Malty to move. Ted swings him outside the leader. He can hear the other jockeys moving toward them from behind. Ted loosens his tight hold on Malty and crouches low. Moving his hands in rhythm with the horse's forward motion, they become a single unit. Ted holds the whip in the palm of his hand. He will use it only if Malty thinks the race is over and stops running.

Malty digs deeply into the track, extending his long forelegs. He comes up even with the leader as they cross the finish line. Ted stands up in the stirrups to signal his horse that the race is over.

Above is an example of a photo finish, showing a triple-dead-heat for "win."

"PHOTO" flashes on the infield board. The Placing Judges will have to decide the winner by looking at an official photograph taken at the finish line.

But to Don, Malty has proven himself. His final desire to push his body to its limits is what every trainer hopes to see in a horse.

Don and Karen are standing outside the winner's circle when Ted rides up. The track announcer makes it official, "The winner, Chocolate Malt, a bay colt by Malta out of Chocolate." Ted slides off Malty's back. Karen gives Malty a happy hug on the neck, then leads him off toward the laboratory shed for tests. Ted shakes Don's hand. "You've got a tryer there, for sure," he says.

That is just what Don has been waiting to hear.

RACING HONORS

The most famous races in the United States are for three-year-olds — the Kentucky Derby, Preakness and Belmont Stakes. If a horse wins all three, it is called a Triple Crown winner.

The highest honor a horse can win is that of the Eclipse Award Horse of the Year. To gain this title, a filly, colt, or older horse would have to stand out as the best runner in the country.

Don has his hopes pinned on Malty. But there is a long way to go. For now he will enjoy the happiness of being the trainer of a two-year old who has just won his maiden race.

GLOSSARY

APPRENTICE - Jockey in his first year of riding.

ASSISTANT STARTER - Person who leads a horse into gate and steadies it until the gate is open.

BREEZE - Fast workout for a short distance.

BROODMARE - Mother horse.

CLERK OF SCALES - Weighs jockeys before and after race with their gear.

CLOCKER - Person who times horses during workouts and races.

COLT - Male horse under five years of age.

CONDITION BOOK - The book issued by the Racing Secretary which explains the rules and conditions for entering a horse in a particular race.

DEAD HEAT - Race in which more than one horse crosses the finish line at the same time.

FILLY - Female horse under five years of age.

FOAL CREEP - Low feeding stall into which only a small horse can fit.

FURLONG - Measure of distance on a race track equal to one-eighth of a mile.

GELDING - A male horse whose sex has been neutered to calm wild behavior.

GROOM - Trainer's employee who takes care of a horse from morning until night.

HALTER - A harness that fits over a horse's head. A rope can be attached to the halter to control the horse.

HAND - Unit used to measure horse's height, equal to four inches.

HOMEBRED - Horse whose owner has bred it to race for his stable, rather than selling it at a yearling sale.

JOURNEYMAN - Jockey with experience.

MARE - Female horse over five years of age.

PADDOCK - Area on race track grounds where horses are saddled before the race.

PATROL JUDGE - Person who watches the race from a tower above the track to be sure neither jockeys or horses commit any fouls.

PLACING JUDGE - Person who decides the order of finish in a close race.

RACING SECRETARY - Designs the races at the track to fit the kind of horses who are stabled there.

REINS - Lines, attached to the bit in the horse's mouth, which are used to guide the horse.

SILKS - Shirt and cap which the jockey wears, usually made of nylon in the owner's colors.

SPRINTER - Horse which races best at distances less than a mile.

STALLION - Father horse.

STAYER - Horse which races best at distances more than a mile.

WALKOVER - If other horses in a race do not show up, the unchallenged horse needs only to "walkover" the course to win. Slang for an easy race.

THE
HORSES
PASTURE TO PADDOCK

CRESTWOOD HOUSE